D1483458

TEMPERATE FOREST MAMMALS

A TRUE BOOK

by
Elaine Landau

Children's Press®
A Division of Grolier Publishing

New York London Hong Kong Sydney
Danbury, Connecticut

A raccoon plays in the forest.

For Michael—
our light in the forest

Reading Consultant
Linda Cornwell
Learning Resource Consultant
Indiana Department of
Education

Subject Consultant
Kathy Carlstead, Ph.D.
National Zoological Park
Smithsonian Institution

Library of Congress Cataloging-in-Publication Data

Landau, Elaine.
    Temperate forest mammals / by Elaine Landau.
        p. cm. — (A true book)
    Includes bibliographical references and index.
    Summary: Describes five different mammals which live in temperate
forests, including raccoons, echidnas, and koalas.
    ISBN 0-516-20043-7 (lib.bdg.)   ISBN 0-516-26115-0 (PBK.)
    1. Forest animals—Juvenile literature. 2. Mammals—Juvenile
literature. [1. Forest animals. 2. Mammals.] I. Title. II. Series.
QL112.L35   1996
599—dc20   96-3889
                                                           CIP
                                                           AC

Contents

The temperate forest is full of life.

Temperate Forests

Imagine living in a forest—a place filled with trees, shrubs, and mosses. Temperate forests are found in areas that have warm summers and cold winters. Some temperate forests have evergreen trees. Some have trees that lose their leaves in the fall. And

Trees in some temperate forests lose their leaves in the fall.

some have a mixture of both kinds of trees.

If you lived in a temperate forest, you would not be alone. Many animals make their homes here. Most temperate forest animals are small. Smaller animals can move easily through the trees and the lower plant growth to find food and shelter.

Living in a forest would mean you might have to face dangerous predators. And your home might be destroyed to make room for farms or apartment buildings. This book introduces a few of the temperate forest mammals. Mammals are animals with backbones and with larger brains than other types of animals. They are also the only animals that nurse their young. Mammals in the temperate forest are affected greatly by what happens to their environment.

Some trees keep their leaves
through the winter.

NORTH
AMERICA

Beavers are
found in
North
America,
Europe,
and Asia.

CENTRAL
AMERICA   Panama

Costa
Rica

EU

AFR

SOUTH
AMERICA

Northern raccoons live in North and Central
America. Crab-eating raccoons are found in
South America, and Costa Rica and Panama.

N
W   E
S

ANTAR

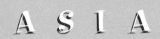

ROPE

ASIA

CA

Echidnas
are found
in Australia
and New
Guinea.

New
Guinea

Wild boars
are found in
Asia, Africa,
and Europe.

AUSTRALIA

Koalas are
found
in Australia.

TICA

Beavers live near lakes or rivers.

Beavers

Beavers are brown, furry rodents. They usually live in colonies along rivers, lakes, and streams in or near forests. Large beavers are about 4 feet (1.2 meters) long and weigh up to 70 pounds (32 kilograms). They have stocky bodies, paddle-shaped tails, short

A beaver's paddle-shaped
tail is helpful in swimming.

limbs, and webbed hind feet.
Beavers have twenty teeth,
including four strong curved
upper and lower front teeth,
called incisors. Unlike those
of humans and most other
mammals, the beaver's incisors
grow throughout its life.

14

Beavers are among the largest rodents on earth today, but they are small compared to their ancestors. Thousands

Trees cut down by beavers

Beavers build lodges in water.

of years ago, North American
beavers grew almost as big as
a bear. Scientists are still not
sure what became of those
huge rodents.

Beavers in the wild live in woodlands, which supply all their needs. They eat plants, tree bark, leaves, roots, twigs, and shrubs. Beaver families also use forest materials to build dams and the teepee-shaped lodges they live in. Beavers work long and hard at these tasks—that's where the phrase "busy as a beaver" comes from.

Bears, wolves, otters, and other animals, including humans, prey on beavers.

When a beaver senses danger, it slams its tail on the water to warn the others in its family. Then it dives to safety beneath the water. A beaver can remain underwater for as long as fifteen minutes.

A beaver's strong front teeth are useful in gnawing tree branches.

These able swimmers were once hunted for their fur. Beavers were important to the fur trade in the 1600s.

The United States and Canada have passed laws to protect these animals. Today, beavers can be hunted only at certain times of the year.

Echidnas

The echidna is an unusual mammal. It is one of only two mammals on earth, including the platypus, that does not give birth to live young. It lays eggs, and its babies hatch from the eggs.

The echidna measures 12 to 24 inches (30 to 60 centimeters) long and weighs up to 22

An echidna has sharp spines and a long snout.

pounds (10 kg). Sharp, pointed spines jut out from the top and sides of its brown coat. It has short, strong limbs and extremely powerful claws. At the tip of its long, skinny snout is a tiny round mouth just wide enough for the

Echidnas use their sticky tongues to lick up insects (above); a young echidna (right)

animal to push out its long sticky tongue.

The echidna eats ants and termites. It digs up the nests or mounds of its prey with its sharp claws. Then, it sweeps up the insects with its long tongue. The echidna's skill at digging also serves as a defense against predators. When it detects an enemy, the echidna speedily digs a hole in which to hide.

Female echidnas lay just one egg a year. The egg develops in a pouch on the animal's belly and hatches after ten days. The baby echidna remains in its mother's pouch for about two months. When its spines appear, the young echidna is ready to leave the pouch.

Many think a raccoon's masklike markings make it look like a bandit (above). Raccoons have long, nimble fingers (right).

Raccoons

It would be hard to mistake a raccoon for any other forest creature. Raccoons have black, masklike markings around their eyes and bushy, ringed tails. Their coats are either gray or rusty brown.

Most raccoons are 30 to 40 inches (76 to 102 cm) long

and weigh 10 to 20 pounds (4.5 to 9 kg). They have long nimble fingers and sharp claws.

Raccoons can live in a number of different environments, but they prefer forests with rivers, lakes, or streams nearby. They often make their dens, or homes, in hollow trees or logs. Raccoons usually live alone or in small family groups. They spend most of

Raccoons often find their food in rivers and streams.

the day resting in their dens and hunt for food after dark.

The raccoon's favorite foods include crayfish, crabs, frogs, and fish. It often relies on its sense of touch to capture its prey. Searching in the

Birds' eggs are a meal for a raccoon.

shallowest part of the water, the raccoon moves its fingers along the bottom until it finds something to eat. These animals also eat nuts, acorns, birds' eggs, mice, and grasshoppers.

In cooler climates, raccoons sleep through much of the winter. They eat a lot in the fall and live on their excess fat during the coldest months. But raccoons do not

Raccoons may look like they are washing their food. But researchers believe raccoons tend to handle their food more than most animals. When this occurs in water, it looks like they are washing it.

Raccoons are hunted by cougars.

actually hibernate. When an animal hibernates, its heart rate and temperature drop. Raccoons do not experience these physical changes.

Coyotes, foxes, wolves, cougars, and other animals prey on young raccoons in the wild. Humans also hunt raccoons—for sport and for their fur pelts. Some people keep these intelligent, amusing animals as pets, but this can be dangerous. Older raccoons may be quick to bite or scratch. Raccoons also may carry and transmit twelve known diseases to humans.

Baby raccoons play on a log.

Koalas have soft fur.

Koalas

The koala is a furry animal that looks like a cuddly teddy bear. Most koalas are 24 to 30 inches (60 to 76 cm) tall and weigh up to 35 pounds (16 kg). The animal has large round ears, a hairless nose, and no tail. The fur is gray or brown on its back, and white on its belly.

Koalas live in the eucalyptus forests of Australia, spending most of their time in the trees. Their strong legs and firm grip make them excellent climbers.

Koalas eat eucalyptus leaves and shoots. They usually feed at night and sleep most of the day. Because eucalyptus leaves tend to be juicy, koalas don't need much water.

A newborn koala is extremely small. Shortly after birth, it climbs into a pouch

Koalas are good tree climbers (left). Eucalyptus leaves are a koala's main source of food (right).

on its mother's belly and stays there for about seven months. After leaving the pouch, the young koala, called a joey, rides on its mother's back until it is about a year old. In the past, koalas were plentiful. But this animal was

A young koala develops and grow in its mother's pouch (left). During its first year of life, a koala often rides on its mother's back (right).

hunted for its fur until it was nearly extinct. At the same time, the koala's natural habitat began to disappear. Many eucalyptus forests were cut down to make way for farms, shopping centers, and housing.

Today, laws protect koalas. A number of conservation groups are also working to save this unique "teddy bear" and its environment.

Wild Boars

The wild boar is a large member of the pig family. A male can reach a length of 6 feet (1.8 m) including its tail and weigh up to 450 pounds (204 kg). Females are usually smaller. Coarse bristles and a thin layer of dark brown or gray hair cover the wild boar's

Wild boars are covered with coarse bristles.

A boar wallows in the mud.

body. The animal uses the two sharply pointed tusks on its lower jaw to defend itself as well as to dig up the ground when it searches for food.

Wild boars feed mainly on plants and roots, in addition to nuts and fruits that have fallen from trees. They also eat small animals, birds' eggs, and insects. These animals tend to look for food at night and rest during the day.

Wild boars are usually found in the thickest parts of the forest where the heavy

The wild boar is a relative of the pig.

underbrush shields them from predators. But on hot days, they often cool off by wallowing in a marsh or a muddy waterhole.

These animals have been hunted for sport for centuries. The kings and nobles of Europe formed royal hunting parties to track down wild boars in the forest. In those days, if the king caught anyone killing a wild boar without his permission, they were severely punished. In more recent times, the wild boar was brought to parts of the United States to be hunted for sport.

A wild boar mother and her young

To Find Out More

Here are more places to learn about temperate forest mammals:

Books

Arnosky, Jim. **In the Forest.** Lothrop, Lee & Shepard, 1989.

Fischer-Nagel, Heiderose. **Fir Trees.** Carolrhoda, 1989.

Hickman, Pamela M. **Habitats: Making Homes for Animals and Plants.** Addison-Wesley, 1993.

Lavies, Bianca. **Tree Trunk Traffic.** Dutton, 1989.

Riha, Susanne. **Animals in the Winter.** Carolrhoda, 1989.

Tesar, Jenny. **What on Earth Is an Echidna?** Blackbirch Press, 1995.

Tresselt, Alvin R. **The Gift of the Tree.** Lothrop, Lee & Shepard, 1992.

Wallace, Karen. **Think of a Beaver.** Candlewick Press, 1993.

Organizations

Canadian Wildlife Service
Environment Canada
Ottawa, Ontario, Canada
K1A 0H3
(819) 997-1095

**National Park Service
Office of Public Inquiries**
P.O. Box 37127
Washington, DC 20013
(202) 208-4747
http://www.nps.gov

Sierra Club
730 Polk Street
San Francisco, CA 94109
(415) 776-2211
http://www.sierraclub.org/

**Smithsonian: National
Zoological Park**
3000 block of Connecticut
  Avenue, NW
Washington, DC 20008
(202) 673-4800
*http://www.si.sgi.com/
perspect.afafam/afazoo.
html*

**Zoological Society
of San Diego**
P.O. Box 271
San Diego, CA 92112-0271
*http://www.sandiegozoo.
org/*

Interactive

**Mammals: A Multimedia
Encyclopedia.** National
Geographic Society.
Discover photos, videos,
and sounds of hundreds
of mammals. Ages 7+

Wide World of Animals.
ABC World Reference.
Meet all kinds of animals
and see how they live.
Ages 7+

Beavers
*http://ngp.ngpc.state.
ne.us/wildlife/beaver.html*
Learn all kinds of facts
about this ingenious
animal.

Raccoons
*http://loomcom.com/
raccoons/*
You won't believe how
much information on
raccoons is here!

Important Words

conservation the act of protecting or preserving

dam a barrier to keep the flow of water at a certain level

eucalyptus a large Australian evergreen tree

extinct no longer existing

habitat an animal's environment

incisors upper and lower front teeth

nimble quick in movement

pelt the furry skin of an animal

predator animals that live by hunting other animals

prey an animal hunted by another for food

rodent a gnawing animal

shrub a thick low-growing bush

Index

Meet the Author

Elaine Landau worked as a newspaper reporter, children's book editor, and youth services librarian before becoming a full-time writer. She has written more than ninety books for young people.

Ms. Landau especially likes writing about the wildlife and plant treasures found in forests. As a child she loved tales of enchanted forests, and for her, these rich dark woodlands never lost their mystery and magic.